I0817226

LOS ANGELES DODGERS

Sam Rhodes

Go to www.av2books.com, and enter this book's unique code.

BOOK CODE

AVX27735

AV² by Weigl brings you media enhanced books that support active learning.

AV² provides enriched content that supplements and complements this book. Weigl's AV² books strive to create inspired learning and engage young minds in a total learning experience.

Your AV² Media Enhanced books come alive with...

Audio
Listen to sections of the book read aloud.

Key Words
Study vocabulary, and complete a matching word activity.

Video
Watch informative video clips.

Quizzes
Test your knowledge.

Embedded Weblinks
Gain additional information for research.

Slide Show
View images and captions, and prepare a presentation.

Try This!
Complete activities and hands-on experiments.

... and much, much more!

Published by AV² by Weigl
350 5th Avenue, 59th Floor
New York, NY 10118
Website: www.av2books.com

Library of Congress Control Number: 2017963669

ISBN 978-1-4896-7963-5 (hardcover)
ISBN 978-1-4896-7964-2 (softcover)
ISBN 978-1-4896-7965-9 (multi-user eBook)

Printed in the United States of America in Brainerd, Minnesota
1 2 3 4 5 6 7 8 9 0 22 21 20 19 18

012018
120817

Project Coordinator: John Willis Designer: Nick Newton

The publisher acknowledges Getty Images, Alamy, Newscom, and iStock as its primary image suppliers for this title.

Contents

Infielder Justin Turner hit 21 home runs in the 2017 season.

GO, DODGERS!

Los Angeles, California, is home to Hollywood and beautiful beaches. It also has a historic baseball **franchise**. The Los Angeles Dodgers are one of the oldest teams in baseball. Some of the best players in the game have worn the iconic "Dodger Blue" uniform. The Dodgers are also known as the Boys in Blue. They work hard to make their city and their fans proud.

The Dodgers have a mix of new talent and veteran players. Cody Bellinger made his debut in the MLB in 2017. Yasiel Puig has been with the Dodgers since 2013.

Who Are the Dodgers?

Major League Baseball (MLB) is made up of the American League (AL) and National League (NL). Each league is separated into East, Central, and West **divisions**. The Los Angeles Dodgers play in the NL West Division. After the regular season, the best teams in each division, plus two **wild card** teams, advance to the **playoffs**. The Dodgers have made 31 playoff appearances.

The Dodgers are worth **$2.75 billion**. They are considered one of the **most valuable teams** in baseball.

One early nickname for the team was the Brooklyn Trolley Dodgers. This was due to the many trolley cars that served the borough of Brooklyn.

WHERE THEY CAME FROM

The Los Angeles Dodgers started way back in 1883 as the Brooklyn Atlantics. Between 1884 and 1932, the team had many nicknames. These names included the Grays, Bridegrooms, Grooms, Superbas, and Robins. In 1932, the team was officially called the Brooklyn Dodgers. In 1958, the Dodgers moved to Los Angeles. They have remained the Los Angeles Dodgers ever since.

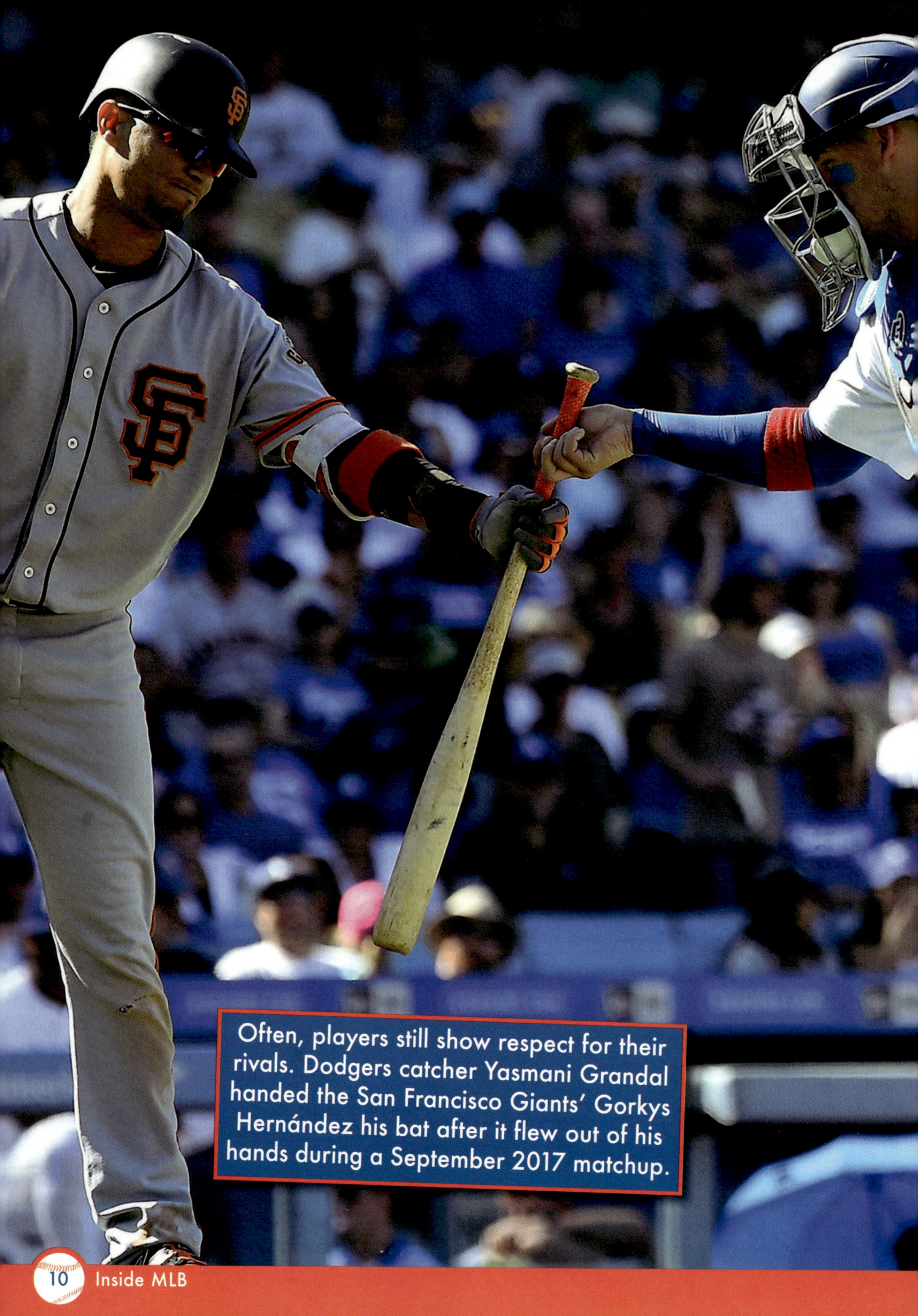

Often, players still show respect for their rivals. Dodgers catcher Yasmani Grandal handed the San Francisco Giants' Gorkys Hernández his bat after it flew out of his hands during a September 2017 matchup.

Who They Play

Every season, each MLB team plays 162 games. The Dodgers play 76 of those games against other teams in their division. The other teams in the NL West Division are the Arizona Diamondbacks, the Colorado Rockies, the San Diego Padres, and the San Francisco Giants. The Dodgers and Giants are big **rivals**. Both teams started in New York and moved to California in the same year!

The **Dodgers** have **won 1,211 of the 2,468 games** played against the **San Francisco Giants** between 1884 and 2017.

Where They Play

Dodger Stadium seats 56,000 fans. It is the main reason the Dodgers moved to Los Angeles. In 1957, Walter O'Malley, the owner of the Dodgers, was unable to make a deal for a new stadium in Brooklyn. Instead, he accepted an offer from the city of Los Angeles. He moved the team in 1958. The stadium took four years to build and opened in 1962. The team still plays there today.

More than **147 million fans** have watched the **Dodgers** play in **Dodger Stadium** since it opened.

After games, news crews set up on the field at Dodger Stadium to interview players, coaches, and managers.

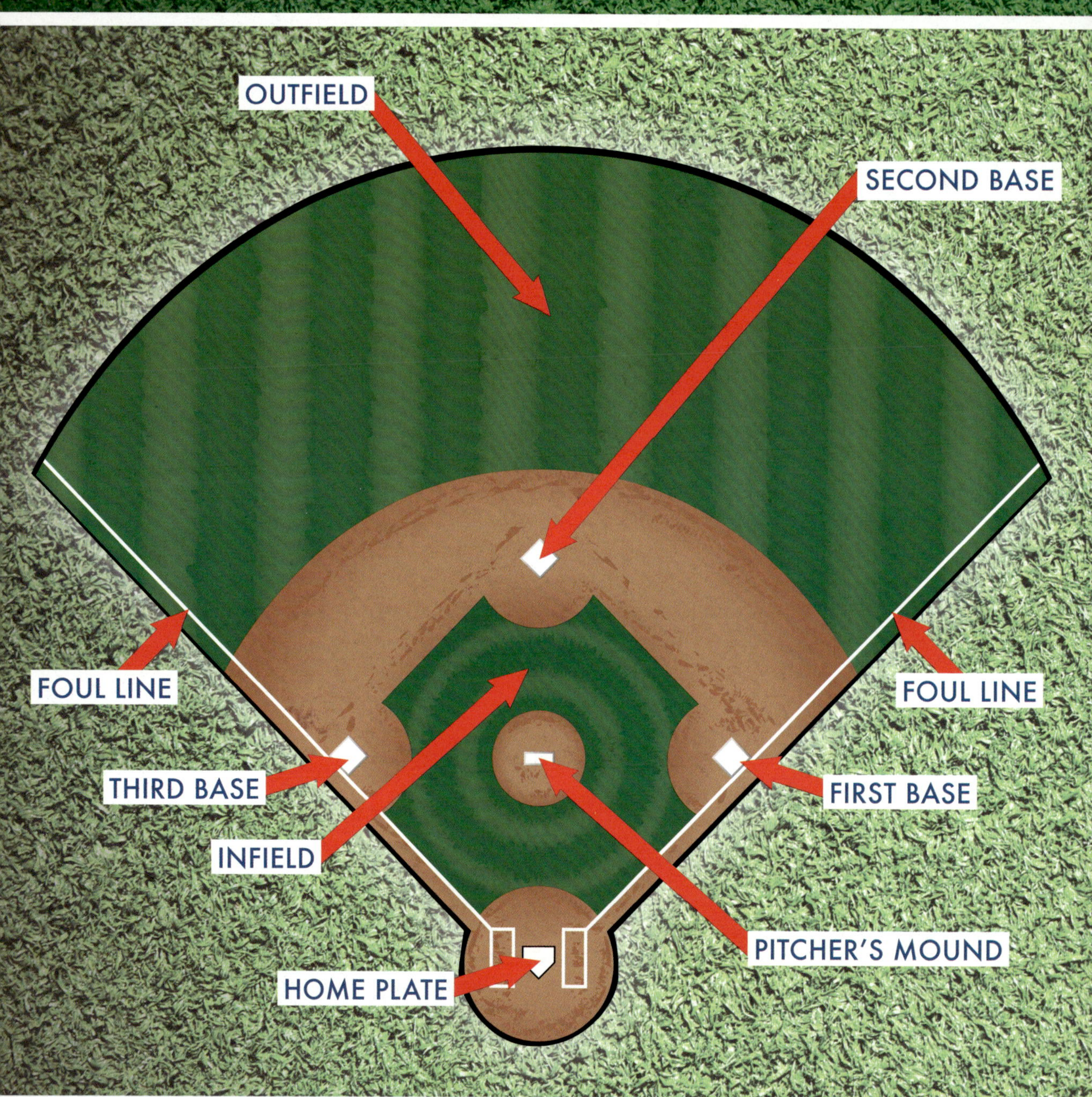
OUTFIELD
SECOND BASE
FOUL LINE
FOUL LINE
THIRD BASE
FIRST BASE
INFIELD
PITCHER'S MOUND
HOME PLATE

THE BASEBALL DIAMOND

Baseball games are played on a field called a diamond. Four bases form this diamond shape. The bases are 90 feet (27 meters) apart. The area around and between the bases is called the infield. At the center of the infield is the pitcher's mound. The grass area beyond the bases is called the outfield. White lines start at **home plate** and go toward the outfield. These are the foul lines. Baseballs hit outside these lines are out of play unless a fielder catches them. The outfield walls are about 300–450 feet (91–137 m) from home plate.

Big Days

The Dodgers have had many triumphs over the course of their long history.

1955: *The Dodgers faced the New York Yankees in the 1955 World Series. History was not on their side. They had lost their last five World Series attempts against the Yankees. This time was different. In the final game of the series, the Dodgers defeated the Yankees 2–0. They won their first* ***championship****.*

1988: *Baseball experts did not expect much from the 1988 Dodgers. The Dodgers defied expectations, though. They made it to the World Series. The Oakland Athletics were favored to win. The Dodgers overcame the odds again and won the championship in five games.*

2017: *The Los Angeles Dodgers finished the 2017 season with 104 wins, more than any other team that year. After dominating the postseason, they faced the Houston Astros in the World Series. The Dodgers lost in Game 7, but proved they were one of the greatest teams in franchise history.*

Joc Pederson hit a home run during Game 6 of the 2017 World Series. In total, the outfielder hit three home runs during the series, with five runs batted in.

Shortstop César Izturis's 2005 season came to a halt in September, when he underwent surgery on his throwing elbow. He had been a contender for the Gold Glove, an annual award given to a player from each defensive position.

Tough Days

Over the years, the Boys in Blue have also seen some tough times.

1924: *The Dodgers had finished in sixth place out of eight NL teams in 1922 and 1923. In 1924, they put in a tremendous effort. Nearing the end of the season, they found themselves leading their division. Ultimately, they could not hold on. They were overtaken by the New York Giants, and just missed the playoffs.*

1966: *MLB champions the year before, the Dodgers breezed through the 1966 season. They made it to the World Series again, but this time they collapsed. They were swept by the Baltimore Orioles, losing all four games of the series.*

2005: *The 2005 Dodgers had the best season start in franchise history. They won 12 of their first 14 games. However, as the season wore on, the Dodgers wore out. Injuries disabled 24 players that season. The Dodgers finished in fourth place, with 91 losses and only 71 wins.*

MEET THE FANS

The Dodgers are one of only three MLB teams with no mascot. The closest thing they have had to a mascot was legendary sportscaster Vin Scully. Scully's warm and cheerful voice was a fixture at Dodger Stadium. He announced all home games from 1950 to 2016, when he retired. However, Dodgers fans still show up in droves to cheer on their team. They led the NL in game attendance from 2013 to 2017.

More than 3 million fans have visited Dodger Stadium each year since 2012.

Pee Wee Reese played for the Dodgers for his entire 16-year MLB career.

Jackie Robinson, Second Baseman

Heroes Then...

The Dodgers have always had fantastic players. Pitcher Dazzy Vance led the NL in strikeouts every year from 1922 to 1928. Shortstop Harold Henry "Pee Wee" Reese was a great batter and base runner in the 1940s and 1950s. Second baseman Jackie Robinson broke the color barrier as the first African American signed to a major league team. He played for the Dodgers in Brooklyn from 1947 to 1956. Robinson was a great all-around player. In 1949, he had the best batting average in the NL. He also helped the Dodgers win their first World Series in 1955. Sandy Koufax pitched for the Dodgers in Brooklyn and Los Angeles. He played from 1955 to 1966. He was the first person to win a **Cy Young Award** three timcs, in 1963, 1965, and 1966. He retired at age 30. Six years later, he was the youngest man ever inducted into the National Baseball **Hall of Fame**.

Heroes Now...

The Los Angeles Dodgers currently have a remarkable roster. Pitcher Clayton Kershaw is arguably the best pitcher in baseball today. He is a three-time Cy Young Award winner. He had the best earned run average (ERA) in baseball from 2011 to 2013, and he has played in the **All-Star Game** every year since 2011. Third baseman Justin Turner has steadily improved his batting since his debut with the Dodgers in 2014. He won the NL Championship Series **Most Valuable Player (MVP)** in 2016. He was also a 2017 All-Star player. Shortstop Corey Seager is a promising young player. He won Rookie of the Year in 2016. Playing first base, Cody Bellinger ranked second in the NL in home runs in 2017. This was his rookie year! Right fielder Yasiel Puig is a solid batter. He helped take the 2017 Dodgers to the World Series.

The present-day Dodgers are loaded with star players.

Clayton Kershaw, Pitcher

Justin Turner, Third Baseman

Corey Seager, Shortstop

GEARING UP

Baseball players all wear a team jersey and pants. They have to wear a team hat in the field and a helmet when batting. Take a look at Austin Barnes and Curtis Granderson to see some other parts of a baseball player's uniform.

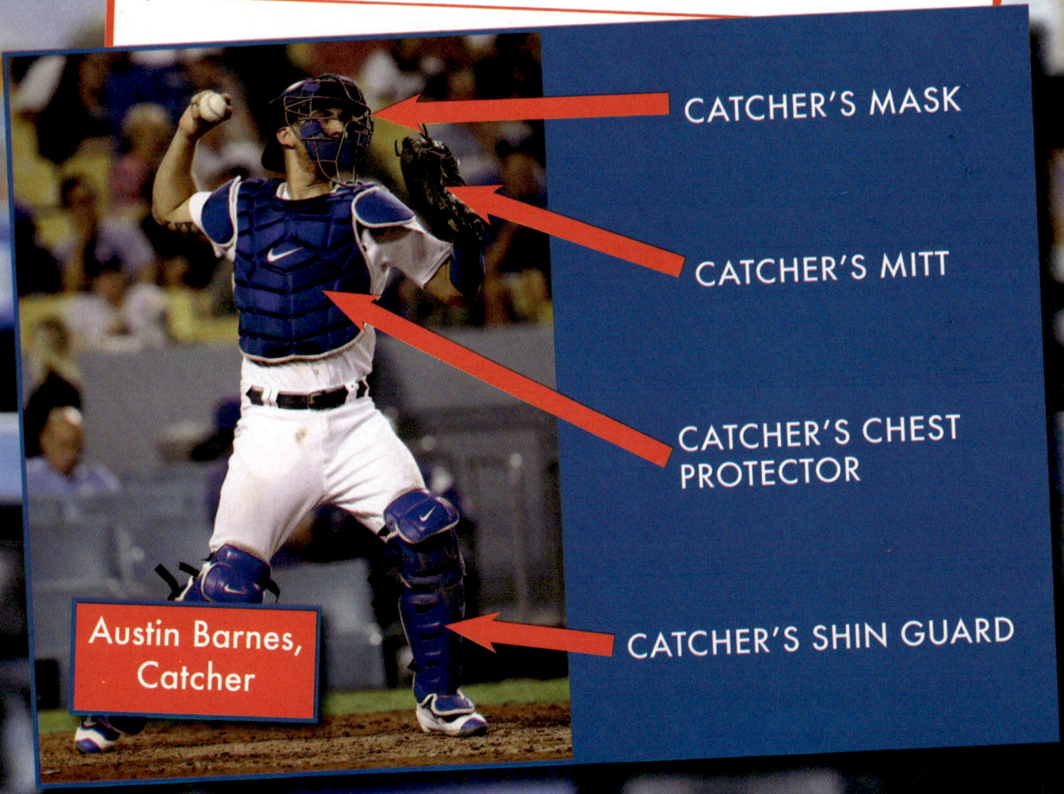

CATCHER'S MASK

CATCHER'S MITT

CATCHER'S CHEST PROTECTOR

CATCHER'S SHIN GUARD

Austin Barnes, Catcher

BAT
BATTING HELMET
BATTING GLOVES
TEAM JERSEY
TEAM PANTS
Curtis Granderson,
Outfielder
BASEBALL CLEATS

SPORTS STATS

Here are some all-time career records for the Los Angeles Dodgers. All of the stats are through the 2017 season.

A Major League baseball weighs about **5 ounces** (142 grams). It is **9 inches** (23 centimeters) around. A leather cover surrounds **hundreds** of feet of string. That string is wound around a small center of **rubber** and **cork**.

Home Runs

Duke Snider, **389**

Gil Hodges, **361**

Runs Batted In

Duke Snider, **1,271**

Gil Hodges, **1,254**

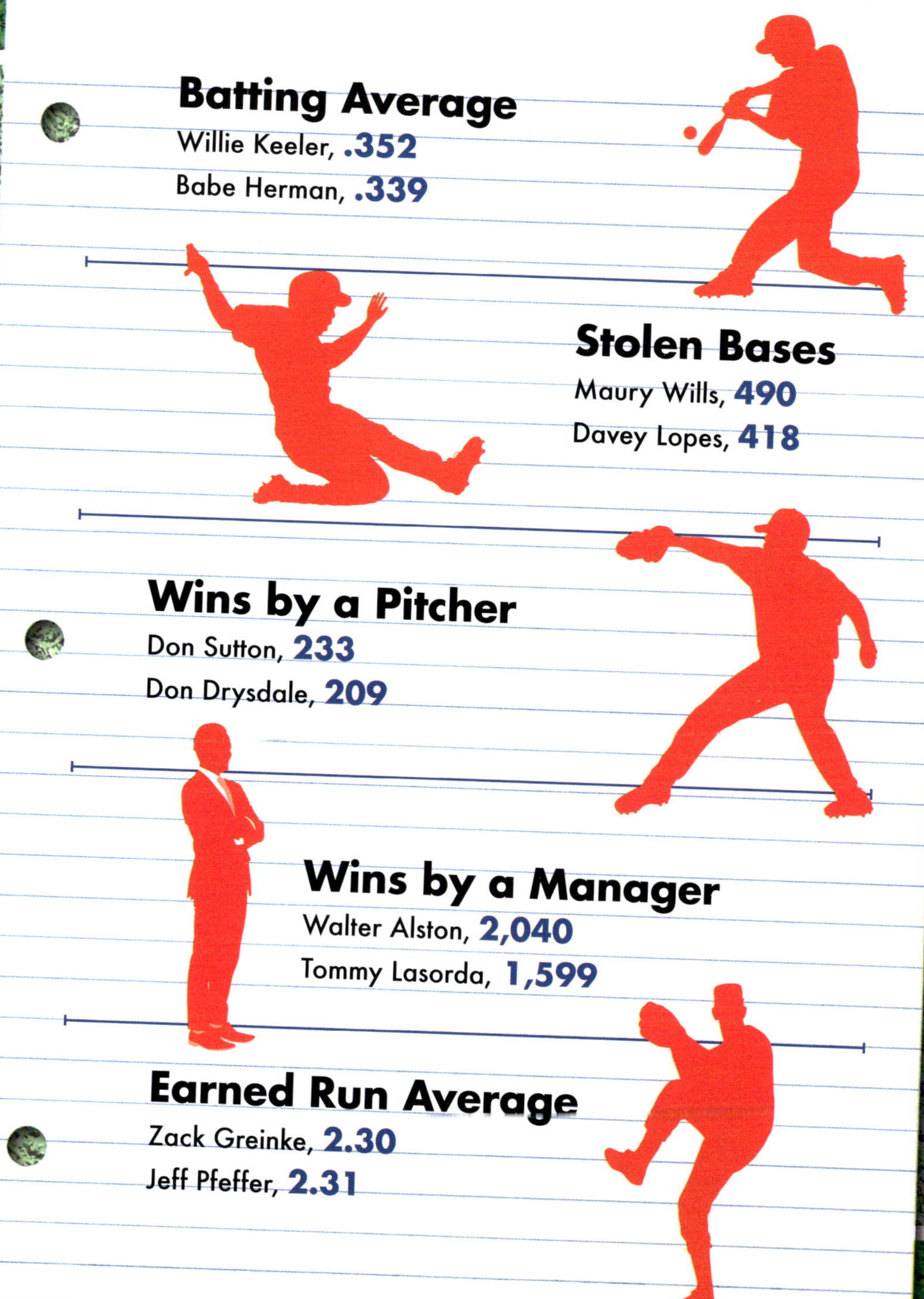
Batting Average
Willie Keeler, .352
Babe Herman, .339
Stolen Bases
Maury Wills, 490
Davey Lopes, 418
Wins by a Pitcher
Don Sutton, 233
Don Drysdale, 209
Wins by a Manager
Walter Alston, 2,040
Tommy Lasorda, 1,599
Earned Run Average
Zack Greinke, 2.30
Jeff Pfeffer, 2.31

1. The Dodgers are also known by what nickname?
2. The Dodgers have made how many playoff appearances?
3. In what year did the team move from Brooklyn to Los Angeles?
4. What word is commonly used to describe the shape of a baseball field?
5. Which team did the Dodgers face in the 2017 World Series?
6. Who was the first person to win the Cy Young Award three times?
7. What is the piece of gear a catcher wears around his lower legs called?
8. Which Dodgers player has the most home runs?

Answers

1. The Boys in Blue
2. 31
3. 1958
4. Diamond
5. The Houston Astros
6. Sandy Koufax
7. A shin guard
8. Duke Snider

Key Words

All-Star Game: an annual midseason game in which the best players from the AL and NL play against each other

championship: one or more games that decide which team is the best

Cy Young Award: an annual award given to the best pitcher in each league

divisions: groups of teams that form one part of a professional sports league

franchise: a team that belongs to a professional sports league

Hall of Fame: a museum that memorializes and honors outstanding people in a particular field, such as sports, science, or art

home plate: the base where a batter stands and where a runner must touch to score a run

Most Valuable Player (MVP): an annual award given to one player from each league

playoffs: the additional games played after the regular season to determine an overall champion

rivals: teams that have a strong sense of competition with each other

wild card: a team, other than the top teams, that also qualifies for the playoffs

Index

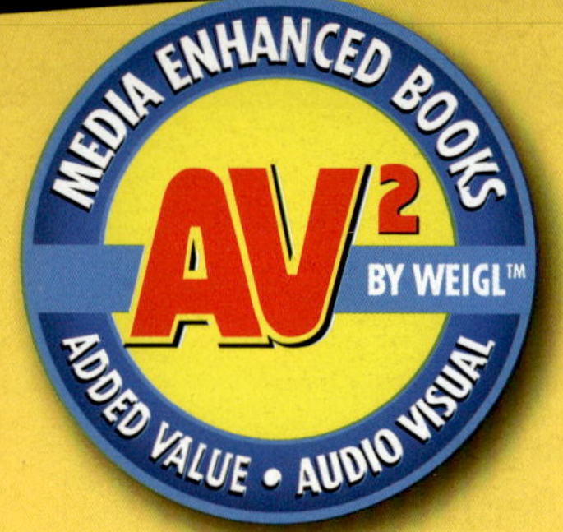

Log on to www.av2books.com

AV² by Weigl brings you media enhanced books that support active learning. Go to www.av2books.com, and enter the special code found on page 2 of this book. You will gain access to enriched and enhanced content that supplements and complements this book. Content includes video, audio, weblinks, quizzes, a slide show, and activities.

AV² Online Navigation

Audio
Listen to sections of the book read aloud.

Book Pages
AV² pages directly correspond to pages in the book.

Video
Watch informative video clips.

Embedded Weblinks
Gain additional information for research.

Key Words
Study vocabulary, and complete a matching word activity.

Try This!
Complete activities and hands-on experiments.

Quizzes
Test your knowledge.

Slide Show
View images and captions, and prepare a presentation.

AV² was built to bridge the gap between print and digital. We encourage you to tell us what you like and what you want to see in the future.

Sign up to be an AV² Ambassador at www.av2books.com/ambassador.

Due to the dynamic nature of the Internet, some of the URLs and activities provided as part of AV² by Weigl may have changed or ceased to exist. AV² by Weigl accepts no responsibility for any such changes. All media enhanced books are regularly monitored to update addresses and sites in a timely manner. Contact AV² by Weigl at 1-866-649-3445 or av2books@weigl.com with any questions, comments, or feedback.